J 972   175760
M
        McNeer, May

        The Mexican Story

            Date Due

JUN 1 6 1970		
3-10-75		

The MEXICAN STORY

BY MAY McNEER

WITH LITHOGRAPHS
BY LYND WARD

Ariel Books · New York

THE DRAWINGS FOR THIS BOOK WERE DRAWN DIRECTLY ON STONE BY THE ARTIST
AND THE BOOK WAS LITHOGRAPHED IN FOUR COLORS BY GEORGE C. MILLER
OF NEW YORK, IN THE UNITED STATES OF AMERICA

ARIEL   BOOKS
IS A DIVISION OF FARRAR, STRAUS AND YOUNG, INC.

CONTENTS

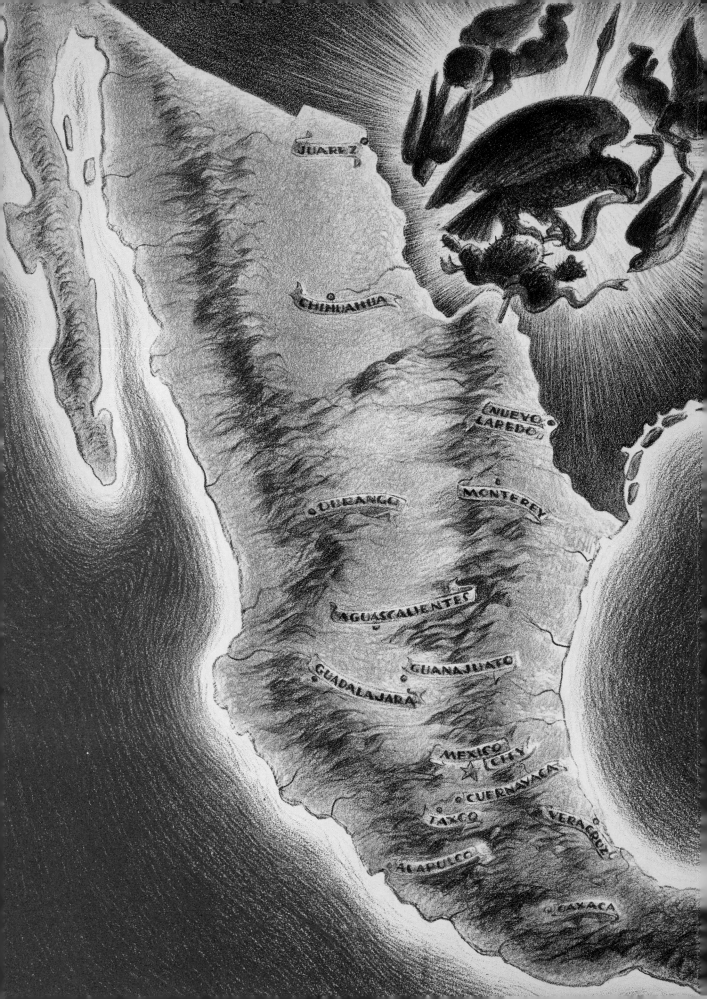

CHAPTER I   UP AND DOWN LAND

MEXICO is a long triangle, pointing to South America. In the north it is a wide land, with many miles of cactus country between the Gulf of Mexico and the Pacific Ocean. But in the south the country narrows as it meets the Central American states.

Mexico is a place of ups and downs. The mountains are breath-takingly steep and high. Some of the great peaks are wild and rugged, and others are planted in orderly plots so far up that they look like patchwork patterns against the sky.

The climate is up and down too. From a cold mountain road, where pines recall Canadian forests, one may look down on warm and humid banana groves and on thatched roofs of huts made of sticks. Mexico has a wet season in summer and a dry season in winter. In the dry months no rain falls, and the steep slopes become brown and gray. When the rains come, water pounds the roofs of mud huts like drumbeats and washes down the mountainsides through deep ravines in a rushing roar. The slopes grow green and flowers spring out all over them. But the rains carry away soil from the mountains and run so fast through the ravines that they do the earth of the lower slopes little good.

The mountains of Mexico contain gold and silver and other minerals. The coastal lands on the Gulf produce oil. And the earth grows strange plants and fruits. The cactus appears as round as a barrel, as pointed as a lance and in great fierce hedges. Maguey is a century plant, ancient and useful, for it gives a drink called pulque as well as rope and food for pigs. It grows only in high altitudes. Sugar cane and corn and cotton grow farther down. And the fruits of Mexico are many — bananas, guavas, mangos, cactus and soft mameys and sapotes, sweet and sticky.

Mexico is a land of flowers and color. It is a land of song and brilliant birds. Snow-topped volcanoes glitter against a sky of vivid blue. Mexico is serene and beautiful, but it can also be unexpected and violent. Only a few years ago a volcano, called Parícutin, thrust abruptly up through a farmer's field while he was ploughing. It quickly buried a village under lava and ashes. A lake once covered a town, and the church spire may be seen by looking straight down into the water from a boat. Mexico is a land where anything can happen.

CHAPTER II   THE PLUMED SERPENT

IN THE early days, there were two great Indian races in Mexico. These
were the Mayas of Yucatán in the south, and the Toltecs in central
Mexico. The Mayas were highly skilled in arts and crafts. They built
great stone cities and temples. From them the Toltecs learned to build,
and they also constructed wonderful carved stone cities and temples in
the shape of pyramids. Then into the Valley of Mexico, which is really
a high plateau surrounded by mountains, came tribes of Nahua Indians.

One of these tribes from the north was called Aztec. The Aztecs had been told by their sorcerers to settle where they found a certain sign. When they came to a salt lake called Lake Texcoco, they saw an eagle perched on a cactus, eating a snake. This was a sign. So, on an island in the lake, they built their huts. The Aztecs were warlike people, but skillful in organizing. They gradually became masters of Mexico. After subduing most of the other tribes, they took over the ways of the Toltecs and began to build in stone. They adopted the gods of the Toltecs too, and of these Quetzalcoatl was the greatest.

This god took his name from the *quetzalli*, or bird of paradise, and the coatl, meaning serpent. He was said to be a tall man with a white skin and a golden beard. The Aztecs believed that Quetzalcoatl, the Plumed Serpent, created man. According to their legends, he gave man corn to grind and eat and taught him to make mats and bowls, to weave cotton into garments and bright feathers into cloaks. The Aztecs said that Quetzalcoatl invented their calendar, which was carved on a huge stone. The god told his people to worship him on the tops of stone pyramids. He gave them laws to live by, trained priests to teach them and, while Quetzalcoatl lived among them, the people knew neither hunger nor fear.

But the enemy of the Plumed Serpent was his brother, Smoking Mirror, the moon god. He persuaded Quetzalcoatl to swallow a magic drink. Quetzalcoatl knew that he had been harmed and could do no more good on earth. He must now return eastward to the land of the gods.

Quetzalcoatl put on his green feather headdress and his snake mask. He promised that in a year of the morning star, called "one reed" on the Aztec calendar, he would return. Then the god went east until he came to the great salt waters. There, on the shore, he made a boat of serpents' skins and sailed away.

After the god had left Mexico, the corn did not grow so high, dry winds from time to time came to ruin the crops, and people were not so well fed nor so happy. But in springtime they dropped grains of yellow corn into the earth. In summer they saw green leaves bending in the winds which came from beyond the snowy volcanoes. In autumn they gathered their corn and feasted and sang of their god, the Plumed Serpent, who would return someday.

CHAPTER III   AN AZTEC MARKET

IN TENOCHTITLÁN dawn came softly, as if to ease the fears of the people who had, not long since, felt an earthquake shake their houses. The
city awoke as usual with the small noises of the dawn. A cock crowed
loudly. A dog barked, and then another answered. A fretful baby
wailed sleepily. A paddle swished softly alongside a canoe. Fires were
built for breakfast, and all across the island city the brown hands of
Indian women moved around and around on the hollowed lava stones,
grinding corn.

It was not quite light when Flower Girl, a little Aztec, opened her eyes with a feeling of excitement. She thought, in a sudden panic, of the earthquake. Then, after that, she had slept, and today was market day in Tenochtitlán. In the entrance to their small mud hut, she could see her mother grinding the corn. As Flower Girl rose quickly from her straw mat she heard the familiar slap slap of her mother's hands. Mother made the tortillas of corn meal, moistened with lime water. Then she patted them on a stone cut from lava.

Flower Girl ran out on her bare brown feet, calling, "May I gather the flowers now?"

She could see her father loading ears of corn into his canoe. He had picked them from one of their floating gardens. The one on which the family had built a hut was firmly fastened to the shore, and it did not move up and down in the small, wind-swept waves as did the other two. Flower Girl jumped from their stationary home-island to the corn garden and then to the flower raft. She drew a deep breath of delight. Dawn was a pale gray now, and she could smell the spicy perfume of crimson carnations and clover blossoms while she moved among the plants, gathering bunches of the dewy flowers.

The early sun cast its first golden light over the city as the canoe loaded with corn and the canoe loaded with flowers started out. Following quickly behind her father, Flower Girl and her mother paddled swiftly and silently through the canals toward the big market. They joined others moving in the same direction. They were part of a great stream of people pouring into the center of the city. Along the wide stone causeways trotted men with huge loads on their backs. The canals were filled with boats. Flower Girl glanced curiously into doorways as she passed by. People were still sleeping on mats on the floors or eating tortillas in the green patio gardens. Some were already at their weaving and pottery making.

Flower Girl and her mother slid their canoe in among many others and tied it up near the market. Father was already unloading his corn there to take to the grain corner of the market.

Carrying their flowers, the two located a spot in the flower corner. There they arranged their blossoms for sale. Around them, friends called out with smiles and friendly greetings. Mother sat down and began to talk to her neighbor. But Flower Girl stood very still.

The market square was large. All around it were buildings with open porches. Here goldsmiths worked on ornaments, and jewelers cut green jade into beads. Over there she heard the pounding on stone of weapon makers, as they fashioned spear tips. Potters were working in clay, and spinners and weavers moved their expert hands, rapidly forming patterns in the cotton cloth which was taking shape on looms.

Flower Girl watched the great moving crowd of nobles and ladies, of merchants, soldiers, farmers and slaves. Her ears were filled with sounds. She heard feather workers calling that their cloaks were the finest ever made. She smelled corn cakes baking, and she listened to the gobble-gobble of turkeys herded through the throng by an old woman with a stick. Everywhere people bargained and bought. Flower Girl saw some being paid with gold dust held in turkey quills for easy carrying and others receiving payment in cocoa beans. Chocolate was the drink of the rich, but the beans themselves served as money for the poor.

Father came over from the grain market and asked Mother to mind the corn for a little. Flower Girl stood alone with her carnations and clover. She arranged them carefully. Yet when the sun rose higher and the day grew warmer, the people who came for flowers seemed to buy more from others. She sold only one small bunch. She was growing tired and hungry but glad, too, that she was not one of the captive slave girls of about her own age passing on the way to the slave market. Gradually as her head began to droop in the heat, she heard a voice say, "They are a little wilted, Mistress."

A fine lady with her slave woman stood before Flower Girl.

"Yes, but they are the best color of any here, and water will bring them up," Flower Girl answered softly, bowing low. "You wish a bunch?"

"No, I will take them all. Gather them up," she ordered her slave, "and let us go. We must find more elsewhere, too, for the feast tonight."

Into the girl's small palm, the slave woman dropped a bag of cocoa beans and moved away, almost hidden behind the flowers that she carried.

Flower Girl could scarcely believe it. She had sold the blossoms— all of them! Smiling, she waited for her mother. Watching a rich man paying for a purchase with gold, she jingled the little bag of beans merrily. These were as good as gold to her, for they would buy a pair of fine turkeys to lay eggs for the family.

CHAPTER IV   MOCTEZUMA

THE CORN grew very tall in the year 1519, the year called "one reed" on the Aztec calendar. One night Moctezuma, the Aztec Emperor and ruler of a number of tribes, went alone to a secret apartment in his palace of many rooms. He had finished his evening meal, served as always by nobles who must come in rags, and barefoot, into the presence of their Emperor. Moctezuma took off his golden ornaments and soft clothing and put on a rough garment of white cotton. He could hear music and laughter sifting in from the apartments where his many wives and slaves lived. He breathed the scent of rare flowers mixed with burning incense. To his ears came the sound of screaming parrots, singing birds in the aviary and the fierce growls and roars of caged animals in his palace zoo.

Suddenly, on an impulse, the Emperor slipped quietly out into the enormous city square. He looked like a poor young noble, unable to wear ornaments because he had not yet reached the lowest rank of military society. Moctezuma knew that his people did not realize that he could ever go about his city in disguise. They thought him a god and fell down to the earth, afraid to look, when he was carried through the streets in his palanquin, or chair with a feathered canopy.

The night had not quite come. The setting sun cast a violet light on the red and white houses of Tenochtitlán, set like a jewel in the lake. Fires flamed upward from pyramidal temples, and a procession of victims being led to sacrifice wound sadly through the plaza.

Moctezuma moved silently into the crowd. Near him stood a young warrior in the jaguar helmet of a military clan, with a red and yellow feather cloak flung about his cotton tunic and padded cotton armor. An old man dressed as a merchant spoke softly to him,

"Ah, but the omens are bad. Perhaps the harvest will be good, if the corn goddess be pleased with the gifts we give her and her son, the Plumed Serpent. But I have just returned from a journey to the south. Everywhere there are evil signs."

The young man nodded his dark head, causing the gold nose and earrings to jingle. "Yes, even though all of our enemies are quiet, except the Tlaxcalans. Indeed we find trouble enough taking captives for our sacrificial fires. They say, too, that the Emperor has so much in his storehouse—fish, flesh, corn, birds and honey, with all kinds of fruits —that the walls are bursting. They say, also, that not enough clerks can be found to write down the tribute from other tribes—gold, jade, featherwork and cotton. Yet I do feel evil. The earth trembled and houses fell not so long ago."

Moctezuma moved silently out of the shadow in which he had been standing and walked along the wide causeway where Indians plodded in from the south, with loads on their backs. He jostled a group of black-

robed priests, with their matted hair and sharp odor of slaughter.

"Nay, this is no time to sleep," he heard one mutter. "We must ask the gods not to be angry. Did you see the column of mysterious fire last night at midnight? And you well know how two temples were destroyed by lightning only some nights ago. It has not been long since the great swirling waters of the lake rose to bear away people and houses from the city."

"The gods are angry. Signs are evil," added another.

Moctezuma, trembling and uneasy, turned and went back to his palace. It was dark now, except for the temple fires. As he returned to his rooms and changed his clothing to the rich garments of the sacred Emperor, he frowned thoughtfully. Then he clapped his hands and asked the noble who bowed before him to order the palanquin. Some of the signs were good this year and some bad. He must know which would prevail.

When the Emperor emerged into the great square, people fell to the stones and hid their faces in fear. He was bourne under the nodding feathers of the canopy past the ball courts and the long racks of skulls.

At the foot of the great temple to the bloodthirsty god of war, Moctezuma got out and, leaning on the shoulders of two of his cousins, climbed the steps to the top. Here he stood in front of the image of the god and looked out over the city. There, beyond the snowy cones of the twin volcanoes, Popocatépetl, the Smoking Mountain, and Ixtaccíhuatl, the Sleeping Woman, he saw a faint light in the sky.

Moctezuma leaned forward, and his hands tightened on the arms of his attendants. His breath caught sharply in his throat. The people of the great city turned their faces up and were silent. A comet flashed its fiery trail across the sky. At that moment the Emperor heard a strange wailing voice of a woman crying, "My children, we are lost!"

When he returned to his palace, his dwarfs and jesters tumbled and joked before him in vain. He sent them all away, even his wise men. Had not his oldest astrologer, who had died several years before, said that the reign of Moctezuma was almost over? More captive slaves were sacrificed to the gods, until the bitter smoke from their burning hearts crept into the palace. Moctezuma trembled. He felt helpless before the wrath of his gods and did not know how to meet the disaster that he believed was coming.

IN 1492, WHEN Aztec power was strongest in Mexico, Christopher Columbus set sail westward across unknown seas. When news arrived in Spain that Columbus had discovered the West Indies, Hernán Cortez was a boy of eight. He grew up with his head filled with tales of voyages and dreams of golden treasures. But Hernán's father did not want his son to be an adventurer. He sent him to college to study law, which Hernán thought a very dull subject. The young man was a born soldier and proved it by leaving law school to join the Spanish Army. He soon became expert in military skills and moved up in rank. By the time he was twenty-six, he was the head of a military district in Cuba. His friend, the governor of Cuba, heard of a rich land westward, reported by a Captain Grijalva, who had just sailed along its coast. He asked Cortez to lead an expedition there.

In 1519, after the eleven ships of the Cortez fleet had dropped anchor off Yucatan, the Spaniards landed and won a battle with the Indians. Then, having learned of other lands to the north, Cortez set sail again to find them. He took with him several slave girls given him by the conquered chieftain. The most intelligent of these was a girl called Malinche. Cortez also took with him a Spaniard named Aguilar who had been held prisoner by the Indians for seven years and who had learned their language. All other members of the crew had lost their lives to the Indians.

At a place on the shore where the city of Vera Cruz now stands, Cortez landed his troops and horses. Along the sandy beach his men spread out, pitching tents, building fires and tethering their animals. Cortez sent exploring parties inland a little way to locate supplies, for food was getting low. When the men returned, however, they were empty handed and reported that they had seen Indians, who had vanished instantly into the forests.

Cortez heard this in silence, frowning, considering ways of getting supplies as he strode up the beach toward the fringe of dark bushes. Suddenly he stopped. Was that a movement? He could see nothing, yet he knew that he was watched by many eyes. Then he noticed a scared brown face among the leaves and soon another and another. Cortez sent for the girl called Malinche and for Aguilar. Malinche could speak the Aztec language, for she had been taken from that tribe as a child, and Aguilar could speak the language of the Maya. Malinche went forward to call to the Indians, telling them that the strangers were friends. Slowly the brown men came out and stood staring at them. Malinche turned to Cortez, while Aguilar translated her words into Spanish.

"These people are in much fear. Years ago their great god sailed away across the seas, promising when he left that some day he would return. They believe that you are that god, the Plumed Serpent, returned to them. They fear you and also the big beasts there, the horses."

Hernán Cortez stroked his reddish beard and smiled. Fortune had been good to him. The Indians thought him a god and the horses supernatural beings. And he had been so lucky as to get a slave girl who spoke the language of the country. He told Malinche to tell the Aztec warriors to advance without fear, and when they had come closer he gave them some small gifts. Then he asked them to bring food.

Soon the white men were feasting on fruits, vegetables and the meat of wild beast and bird. Cortez had found out from the chief, who came to sit in the tent with him, that there was a greater chief far inland. He learned that this Emperor, Moctezuma, lived in a palace on an island in a lake and that he had gold and jewels. Cortez smiled again. Fortune was indeed good to him. He saw the chief looking in wonder at the guns, steel lances and helmets of the troops.

Cortez reached out and took a helmet from the head of one of the men. He gave it to the chief, saying, "Tell your king that the strangers send him greetings. Tell him that, if he is my friend, he will send this helmet back filled with gold dust."

The couriers ran toward Tenochtitlán, passing along from one fast runner to the next both the helmet and a cotton cloth painted with the picture message for Moctezuma. Then Indians appeared on the shore from another tribe. They were friendly to the strangers but showed that they hated the Aztecs. For the Aztecs, who had defeated them, were constantly taking not only taxes but also young men to be killed on the altars of their cruel gods. Cortez enlisted their aid and began to make plans for using the captive tribes against their masters.

When the runner returned and handed Cortez the helmet filled with gold, the white captain's eyes gleamed. He called his officers together and told them what he had in mind—to strike straight at the heart of the Aztec empire and take the capital city itself. This was a dangerous scheme for so few men against so many. But the Spaniards had guns and horses and the hatred of the captive tribes on their side. They also had the advantage of their fear of the gods. Furthermore, Cortez believed that the reward in riches would be worth any risk.

Although the men agreed to go, Cortez was afraid that some might turn back. To make sure that they could not desert, Cortez set fire to the ships. As they watched the flames rise on the water, the men were pale and angry. Their captain shouted to them, "Those ships cannot return! When we have the riches that we came for, we will make new ships."

The men muttered to themselves, but not loudly. It was clear that to follow Hernán Cortez was to give one's life into his hands. There was no turning back.

Cortez had with him six hundred men and sixteen horses. The little

army made its way up mountains so high that the men dared not look down as they climbed. To the south they saw the white cone of Mount Orizaba. They descended into warm tropical valleys filled with jungles, where monkeys chattered and parrots screamed. In the country of the Tlaxcaláns they found hostile Indians and defeated them in battle with the terrifying guns. Then Cortez persuaded the Tlaxcaláns to join him, for these people hated Moctezuma.

Accompanied by a Tlaxcalán army they came to Cholula, a place sacred to the Aztecs. Here they first met Moctezuma's men. The invaders fought the Cholulans in the central square and left the sacred city a smoking ruin, with the dead lying in heaps. Then the Spaniards moved on between the two volcanoes, the Smoking Mountain and the Sleeping Woman, to the royal city.

Moctezuma came out to meet the white strangers. He did not know what to do, for one moment he wanted to set his army against them, and the next he quivered with fear because he believed them to be gods. On the wide causeway he stepped out of his palanquin and welcomed the pale bearded men in steel armor. He led them to a palace on the great square and presented them with gifts.

Cortez knew that he could not keep these people from finding out quickly that the white men were not gods. He must act at once. Taking his most trusted followers with him, he went to the Emperor, as if on a friendly visit, and persuaded Moctezuma to come to the other palace. There Cortez shut him up under guard. All of this took place before

the Aztec nobles were aware of his intentions, for Cortez knew that Moctezuma was weak and afraid, believing the white invaders to be gods. As long as the braver chieftains could be kept away from their Emperor, Cortez was in command of the situation.

Then one of the Spanish guard left at Vera Cruz came with word that a ship had arrived from Cuba, carrying a Captain Narváez, sent by the Cuban governor to replace Cortez. Hastily giving command of the forces in the city to big blonde Captain Alvarado, Cortez hurried back to the coast with some of his men. There he defeated Narváez in battle and persuaded these new troops to join him.

When Cortez returned to Tenochtitlán, he rode into a city that was strangely silent. People had shut themselves inside their houses. In the plaza there were heaps of bodies of Indian nobles. Alvarado had mounted his guns at the entrances of the square, while a religious festival was taking place within and had opened fire on the crowd. Moctezuma was ill in his palace prison and the princes and nobles who had survived had disappeared.

Cortez knew now that the Indians no longer believed him to be the Plumed Serpent. They no longer believed the horses to be supernatural creatures, for in the fighting a horse had been killed. Its head, with that of one of the white soldiers, was hung on a pole before the temple.

Cortez smelled danger all around in the silence. He gripped his sword hilt fiercely but did not give up his intention to conquer this country. He shut himself in his rooms and made his plans.

BESIDE the white conqueror, in his steel armor, there was always the slim brown girl, Malinche. The Spaniards baptized her and renamed her Doña Marina. But to the Indians she was Malinche, and the name came to mean "traitor" to them.

Malinche was a strange girl. When she was little she had been a princess in an Aztec tribal village. Her father died, though, and her mother married again and had a son. Then the mother felt that her daughter was only in the way of the son. So when a wandering group of slave merchants came to the village, the mother sold Malinche to them. They took her south to Yucatan and sold her again to a chieftain. Here she grew up a bitter, lonely girl. Because of her hatred of her own people, she was glad to help the white men.

CHAPTER VII   CUAUHTÉMOC

WITH THE aid of Malinche, Cortez talked to Moctezuma, persuading him to go to the roof of the palace where he was kept prisoner and speak to his people. The Emperor, who was so ill that he was unable to stand, told the silent crowd in the square that Cortez was their conqueror. The answer was a shower of stones. Moctezuma fell under them and had to be carried back to his rooms, where he died soon after.

In the palace on the great square, the Spaniards moved as quietly and as quickly as possible. The furious crowds in the plaza had melted away after word had gone through the city that Moctezuma was dead. Now there was a deadly quiet again. Cortez meant to escape secretly that night. Rain was falling, and there was no moon. Cortez believed that the brother of Moctezuma was rallying his warriors for an attack.

The Spaniards cursed softly while they saddled the horses, and tried to take away as much of their stolen gold as possible. When darkness came, a file of men and horses moved along the shortest causeway to the mainland. Reaching the first of the openings in the causeway, Cortez saw that the Aztecs had removed the bridges. But he had thought of

that ahead of time and had had a portable bridge made and carried with the troops. Cortez intended to have it put over each opening and then raised and brought to the next one.

When the horses clattered across the wooden bridge, they suddenly became aware of dark figures in hundreds of canoes moving alongside. The great snakeskin drum in the temple began to throb — faster and faster. A frightful Indian war cry broke out into the rainy night. Instantly the city was alive. Warriors dashed their lances against the helpless Spaniards and their horses. Stones were hurled from slings and arrows showered on them. Cortez shouted to his men to raise the bridge as the last troops passed over it. But the bridge could not be brought to the next opening. It had been pushed too far down into the mud to be lifted.

Men and horses fell into the water, and others climbed to safety over them. Captain Alvarado, who was one of those in front, thrust his lance into the lake bottom and pole-vaulted in a mighty leap to the other side. When the survivors arrived on the mainland and Cortez saw how few had come across, he sat down beneath a big cypress tree and wept. Ever since that time the tree has been called the Tree of the Sad Night.

Cortez gathered his broken army together and led it to the south. On the plains of Otumba, he was set upon by pursuing warriors from the city. The guns of the white men held off the hordes of Indian fighters for a time, but Cortez knew that they could not do so much longer. As he fought, he suddenly caught sight of the royal green feathers and knew that this was the commander of the enemy. He made a lunge at the prince and with great thrusts of his sword killed him and several of his chiefs. This decided the battle. In confusion the Indians withdrew. Cortez led his men to the east, back to the country of the Tlaxcaláns.

There he was received with friendship and immediately made plans for another attack. First, Cortez sent out parties to take the towns of Xochimilco and Cuanhnahuac, now called Cuernavaca. Then he put the Tlaxcaláns to work in the forests, cutting trees and shaping timbers. In four months' time these workers had made all of the parts for thirteen sailing vessels. On the backs of thousands of Indians these parts were carried over high mountains to the shore of Lake Texcoco. There

they were put together, and the ships launched. Since his supply of gunpowder was scant, Cortez had two of his men lowered by ropes into the crater of a volcano to bring out sulphur to make more. Other supplies were obtained with equal fortitude.

Back in the island city of the Aztecs, the brother of Moctezuma had died during a violent epidemic of smallpox, a disease brought there by one of the Spaniards from Cuba. The leader was now Cuauhtémoc, a nephew of Moctezuma. Cuauhtémoc was a brave and determined man, with none of the weaknesses of his uncle. He made plans for the defense of the city against the relentless Cortez.

Cortez, however, had planned carefully. He cut the ducts that carried fresh water to the city from Chapultepec hill. The waters of Lake Texcoco were brackish and unfit to drink. Then Cortez besieged the island city. He ringed it with his thirteen ships and with their guns prevented Indian canoes from bringing in food. Hunger, thirst and disease helped the Spaniards, for smallpox now raged in Tenochtitlán. Cuauhtémoc and his warriors fought bravely on the causeways and from canoes with arrows, lances and slings. When the Spaniards tried to land, men and women rolled big stones down on them from housetops. Yet the dead piled up in the houses and in the canals.

As Cortez moved slowly into the city, he had all of the buildings leveled to the earth. The final battle was fought in the great temple square. Cuauhtémoc escaped in a canoe when the end came for his forces but was captured on the lake. Cortez promised him the honors due a brave chieftain. Cuauhtémoc, however, refused to tell Cortez where he had buried the royal treasures. Even under torture he said nothing. And so Cortez had him put to death.

When Cuauhtémoc died, the heart of Mexico was conquered. Nevertheless, Cuauhtémoc became the immortal hero of the Indian peoples. His name to them meant courage.

Cortez ordered the dead buried and the city of Tenochtitlán rebuilt on the rubble of its own destruction. It came to be called Mexico City. On the plaza, where so many human victims had been killed to appease Indian gods, the temples were destroyed and a great cathedral was begun. Priests were brought from Spain. In other towns, churches were built on the very spots where the Aztecs had worshipped their strange gods. Indians came to listen to the priests. Gradually the old religion was joined with the new. Indians were baptized by the thousand and Mexico became a Catholic country.

Hernán Cortez was the conqueror of Mexico. After the Aztecs had been overcome he subdued all of the other tribes that resisted him. Spain rewarded him with vast estates in Morelos and Oaxaca and gave him the title of Marquis of the Valley. But the highest office in Mexico, that of viceroy, was not given to Cortez.

He finally retired with his wife and family to a plantation in Morelos where he began the growing of sugar cane. This did not satisfy the famous old military captain for long, so he went on an extended expedition to explore lands to the north. Various calamities, however, overtook his ships, and he did not find any more riches. Instead, he returned to Spain to claim honors and rewards that he felt he should have had. The Emperor received him coldly, for Cortez was no longer of any use to him. Hernán Cortez, with the young son who had accompanied him, went to Seville, where he died in 1547. His son took his father's body back to Mexico to be buried in the land that he had conquered for Spain.

CHAPTER VIII   FRIAR BARTOLOME

FROM THE time of Cortez, Spain owned Mexico. At first Spaniards came to hunt gold, following rumors of hidden treasures. Then, when they had taken all that the Indians had, the Spaniards opened mines for gold, silver, copper and iron. They also began to cultivate big estates and to enslave Indians to work them. They branded the Indians on the face, like cattle, and treated them worse than they treated the animals brought from Europe.

Before the conquest there had been no work animals in Mexico. Now ships from Spain brought donkeys, sheep, horses, cattle and oxen, and the Indians were taught to make wheels and construct wagons. The Spanish government began to send wheat, sugar cane and orange trees to be planted in the fertile soil of the new colony.

During this time, the City of Mexico was being rebuilt by the labor of many slaves. It became a beautiful city again, though very different from the city of Moctezuma. Towns were laid out in other parts of Mexico also, on important roads leading to mines and to the major ports. Mexico became Spanish in language and in custom, at least in the homes of the wealthy. Indians in towns began to speak the new language, although most of the far-away villages remained native in ways and in speech. As in the days of Aztec rulership, the tribes continued to use their own languages.

While some Spanish priests lived like rich nobles and made slaves of the Indians, others, such as Friar Bartolome de las Casas and Bishop Vasco de Quiroga, spent their lives helping the Indians.

Friar Bartolome de las Casas came to Mexico from the West Indian islands, where he had seen natives enslaved and killed in great numbers. Now he saw this happening again in Mexico. He wrote many letters to the Spanish king telling him of the terrible plight of the Indians. He also asked for laws for their protection. But, although some laws were agreed to by the king, they were not enforced in Mexico.

Bishop Quiroga, seeing the great beauty and skill of Indian workmanship, had whole villages taught Spanish handicrafts. Before long, Indians were expert in leatherwork, Spanish pottery and the weaving of wools. He also started several schools for them.

FOR MANY years after 1600, only a few Indian children could go to church schools to learn to read and write. The owners of big haciendas, or ranches, were Spanish or were descendants of the many Spaniards who married Indian girls. They lived in beautiful homes in towns and cities and spent the holidays at their haciendas. Their sons and daughters were taught by tutors or at colleges in Mexico City. These wealthy families formed a social group that was as used to luxury as any royal court in Europe. The men went to cockfights and bullfights and the ladies drove about the parks in the afternoon in formal dresses with diamonds at the ears and throat.

The central figure of this social set was the wife of the Spanish Viceroy, Doña Leonor Carreto. Of all the ladies-in-waiting of Doña Leonor's court, the one who attracted most attention was a slight dark-haired girl, Juana Ines de Asbaje. She had come to the city at the age of fifteen, and already she was writing verses that were witty and graceful.

The Viceroy was delighted with his wife's young friend, for she had a brilliant mind. In a discussion of the classics, Juana Ines would often defeat some of the University of Mexico professors.

One day Juana Ines astonished the court, where she was such a favorite, by announcing that she was going into a convent. At the convent of Saint Jerome she spent most of her time alone, studying and writing. For twenty-five years Sister Ines wrote verses and treatises and became the first famous writer of Mexico.

Then, with another sudden decision, the nun gave away all of her many books. From that day she wrote no more, devoting herself instead to the service to others. When the plague came to the convent in 1695 and many of the nuns were ill, Sister Ines took care of them until she herself died. To her country she left her writings. Today she is called the greatest of Mexican poets.

GOLD DREW men from Spain to Mexico in the 1500's. Yet the eighteenth century was called the Silver Age in Mexico.

In 1717 an adventurous Frenchman called, in Spanish, José de la Borda, wandered into a village perched on the wild mountains south of Mexico City. Here silver had been mined for two hundred years until the surface veins had run thin, and the mining had stopped. Taxco was only a small group of adobe huts on a hillside. Borda, however, discovered that these mountains had deeper and richer deposits of silver ore hidden in them. He put the Indians to mining silver for him and made a fortune.

The little French dandy, in his silken knee breeches and ruffles, rebuilt the village of Taxco. He had the houses constructed in terraces one above the other on steep mountainsides and colored in red and white and green and blue. He had the Indians pave the narrow streets with cobblestones for the small, sure hoofs of burros carrying silver ore. Here, on the main square, or *zocolo* as it is called, he built his own palace for his family. And then he began the construction of a church of red stone, carved and ornamented, with the interior a mass of gilt. Asked why he had spent so much of his fortune on the church, he replied, "God gives to Borda, and Borda gives to God."

When the little silver prince grew tired of his mountain town, he went to live in Cuernavaca, between Taxco and Mexico City. Here he had an estate now called the Borda Gardens, with pools and tropical flowers. Like a king in his own kingdom lived the Frenchman. So much silver came to him that when his daughter married, he had a street paved with blocks of it. The bride walked on silver to her wedding in her father's church of Santa Prisca.

CHAPTER XI   FLACO THE SKINNY ONE

LUPITA was an Indian mountain girl, daughter of a potter. Her father spent his days in the town, forming wet clay with patient hands into bowls and dishes, decorated with graceful birds and flowers of the region. Her mother worked in the household of a rich man, owner of a silver mine in the town of Taxco.

From her small hut made of adobe brick, built high on Taxco's hillside, Lupita could look down on the rose-colored church of Santa Prisca. The day was January 17, 1790. A special date for Lupita, for it was the day of Saint Anthony the Abbott, patron saint of animals.

Lupita wanted to join in the celebration of the Saint's day, but instead she must look for her small brother, Pablo. Already her feet were tired, and her head hurt with worry, though it was yet early morning. Had Pablo wandered into the mountains? Wolves and snakes lived on the rocky hillsides. And where was their donkey, Flaco, the Skinny One? Never mind. Today she could not lead Flaco to the church for the blessing of the animals. She must find Pablo before her mother returned.

Lupita looked and looked. She searched behind every cactus, towering tall and spiny, and behind every boulder, with her ears cocked for the sound of a rattler. Suddenly she saw a small movement far up on the hillside. Lupita ran, stumbling on her sandaled feet, her blue rebosa shawl flying out behind her. Yes, that was the gray tail of Flaco, and yes—that was the small black head of Pablo. Flaco had found the lost

Pablo. Lupita laughed and she scolded, and then she put Pablo on Flaco's back and led them both down to the village.

There the procession was forming. All of the village animals were decorated with white chalk, pink flour and red and blue and purple strips of cloth. Maria, Lupita's friend, ran with her two dogs, their faces painted funnily with pink and white chalk, and thrust some colored streamers at Lupita. Lupita laughed, white teeth suddenly gleaming in her dark face. With hands quick and clever from weaving, she tied bows on the ears of Flaco. Then she led him to the procession.

Lupita stood with her friends and their goats, pigs, dogs and donkeys in the plaza before the beautiful church. She looked up at the rosy towers against the deep blue sky and thanked Saint Anthony for helping her find Pablo and Flaco, the Skinny One. At one side of the square she saw her mother, smiling. She heard the words of the priest blessing the animals. Then Pablo laughed and tweaked the ear of the donkey. Flaco lifted his head and brayed until the echoes rang down the hillside. Everybody laughed, especially Lupita.

CHAPTER XII   CARLOS THE SCIENTIST

IN EVERY town in Mexico in the 1700's the church was the center of life. Every few weeks a religious fiesta was held to bless the animals, celebrate harvests, honor saints or miracles. Often the Indian and the Christian religions were strangely mixed. The only schools were those run by the churches.

In some towns there were schools for boys, taught by Jesuit priests.

There the youths learned, not only religion, but some mathematics along with Latin and Greek. One of the most promising students in a church school was a boy who bent his head constantly over his books and papers. He liked to write. And he put his thoughts so often on paper that his schoolmates laughed at him. When he walked slowly into the church garden and waited with the little group of boys for the schoolroom doors to open, he held his books tightly under his arm. He moved back out of the way as two of his friends tussled in the dust in a friendly struggle. Father Jerome pulled open the big doors. The boys straightened their smocks and stood quietly, shuffling their feet a little.

The priest glanced at them. "I see that Carlos has not forgotten his books today."

One of the boys raised his eyebrows and laughed. "But Carlos wears his head in the clouds, Father."

"The only clouds around you, José are clouds of dust. Carlos will be a scholar some day."

Carlos grew up to be Don Carlos de Sigüenza, a professor at the University of Mexico, the oldest university in the Americas. There he made a name for himself with his astonishing ability in mathematics, astronomy and history. He also earned the disapproval of the Church by claiming that comets were not of divine origin but were due to natural laws.

Don Carlos had always been interested in the ancient stone pyramids of the Indians. While he was still in school, he had picked up stone pieces used as spear points by the Aztecs against the Spanish invaders. Often he turned over and over in his hands a curiously carved piece of jade or obsidian, wondering what it meant. When Don Carlos became a professor, he began to study the ruins of Mexico and to learn from them of the wonderful tribal knowledge recorded on stone.

Before he died, Don Carlos was known in Europe and was considered the first scientist of Mexico. New ideas began to grow in his country, in politics as well as in science. Mexico was still a Spanish colony. But when the Mexicans began to hear of the breaking away of the English colonies in North America and of the formation of a new nation there, they began to hope for their own freedom as a separate country, too. Independence did not seem impossible.

IN THE state of Querétaro, in the early 1800's, a little group of thought-ful people gathered at the home of the governor. His wife, Doña Josefa Ortiz de Dominguez, was the most popular hostess outside Mexico City. All of the notables who passed through the state stayed at her house. And the people who lived at the big haciendas came for many miles to enjoy her hospitality.

In the drawing rooms of Doña Josefa, ladies and gentlemen sat on high-backed carved Spanish chairs and drank frothy chocolate from thin cups. They talked of the injustices suffered by Mexicans in a Spanish colony. Only Spaniards born in Spain could hope to rise to high government positions or important offices in the church.

Doña Josefa, moving quietly in her elegant silk gown, welcomed guests and kept the conversation going. She often invited priests and officials, doctors and lawyers and visiting military officers. But she was most interested in the beliefs of a priest who lived in a village not far away. His name was Father Hidalgo. He was not only interested in freedom from Spain, but he also wanted more food and better conditions for the Indians. Doña Josefa shared his beliefs.

Another friend of Doña Josefa and Father Hidalgo was Captain Allende of the Royal Guards. When the other guests left, one by one, Captain Allende and Father Hidalgo often stayed late talking of the problems of their country. The idea of freedom for Mexico was sweep-ing through the land like a strong wind from the mountains. In fact, the idea was becoming a plan for action in the minds of these people who sipped chocolate in the drawing room of Doña Josefa.

CHAPTER XIV   FATHER HIDALGO

FATHER HIDALGO was the son of an old Spanish family but born in Mexico. He was a priest and had been rector of the College of San Nicolás in the town of Valladolid. But he gave up his teaching to become the parish priest in the village of Dolores, where the people

had scarcely enough to eat. Like his people, he was very poor. Day after day, he watched the endless, losing struggle for food, until he felt he must help. He persuaded some of his wealthier friends to send for grapevines and mulberry trees, and then he showed the Indians how to cultivate them. He got a few silkworms and placed them in the mulberry trees, thinking that it would be good for these people to grow silk.

Mexico, however, was under Spanish rule. Mexicans were not allowed to raise grapes and make wine, or grow mulberry trees and silkworms. Only the Spanish in Spain could have these privileges, and Mexicans must buy the products from Spain. The government sent men to Dolores to destroy all of the plants so carefully tended by the Indians. Then Father Hidalgo thought of the potter's trade and he went away to learn it. When he returned, he showed his people how to mould clay into jars and vessels of all kinds. Since this took time, the craft was not easy to start. People were still hungry and without enough clothing. Father Hidalgo became more angry at Spain for keeping Mexico a colony. He believed that Mexico must have her freedom from Spain.

At Doña Josefa's home, plans were made for a revolt. It was to start on December 8, 1810. But one night in September, Doña Josefa heard that someone had betrayed the plans to the authorities. Quickly she sent word to Father Hidalgo. He called his fellow leaders, including Captain Allende, and they decided to act. While Father Hidalgo walked back and forth, pondering the problem, the thought of the Virgin of Guadalupe, beloved shrine of the Indians, came to him. He remembered the story of the saint.

On a little hill near Mexico City, there had once been a statue to the Aztec Goddess who was the mother of the Plumed Serpent god. One day, in 1531, as a poor Indian named Juan Diego was crossing this hill, he heard music and a lovely voice calling his name. Then he saw a vision of the Virgin, who told him to tell the bishop that she wanted a church to be built on that hill. Juan went to the bishop, who refused to listen to him, asking him instead to bring proof. Juan went back and the Virgin spoke to him again, telling him to go up on the bare hillside and pick some roses for the bishop. Juan climbed among thorns and stones and cactus plants and was amazed to find roses blooming there. He gathered them into his cape and took them to the bishop. When the cape fell open, there beneath the roses was a picture of the Virgin.

The Virgin of Guadalupe was the patron saint of the Indians, who believed that she especially loved the poor. Father Hidalgo decided to ask the blessing of the saint for his attempt to free Mexico from Spanish rule.

He strode to the church steps and grasped the bell rope. Clang, clang, clang! People came running from their houses to gather before the church. Father Hidalgo prayed to the saint and then spoke to the people of Dolores, ending with a great shout, "Down with the bad government! Long live the Virgin of Guadalupe!"

Then he started through the streets, followed at first by only sixteen men armed with machetes, the broad-bladed knives that the workers used for cutting sugar cane, and with sticks and slings. All along the way more people joined them. They went to other villages and towns, and everywhere people poured out to go with them. Before long, Father Hidalgo and Captain Allende had an army of wild and vengeful men. Within two months there were almost a hundred thousand in this ragged army. They seized Spanish estates, opened jails, freed slaves and fought battles with government troops. Father Hidalgo began to plan for a congress for his new administration and to think of a ruler for Mexico. Independence seemed very close.

The church authorities were terrified. They declared that Father Hidalgo was no longer a priest, and the government placed a price on his head. Troops were sent in larger number to stop the revolt against Spain. But the ragged army, fighting under the banner of the Virgin of Guadalupe, defeated government troops in battle after battle. Then came the question of an invasion of Mexico City. Captain Allende was for it, but Father Hidalgo did not take his advice. He hesitated too long. Many of his followers became impatient and deserted. Government forces captured some of his artillery, and in the next battle the Hidalgo army was defeated. Captain Allende and two other leaders were shot as traitors to Spain.

Father Hidalgo was deprived of his priestly robes and was executed, but he has for many years been honored as the father of his country. He tried to free Mexico from Spanish rule. The day of his revolt is celebrated now in Mexico City by a great festival, when the people assemble in the huge plaza before the cathedral and the presidential palace. The President of Mexico rings the freedom bell, taken to the palace from the church of Father Hidalgo in Dolores. Then he gives the call, known as *the grito* or *El Grito de Dolores*. But it has been changed. The president cries, "Mexicans, long live our heroes! Long live independence! Long live Mexico!" The people take up the cry— and all through the republic, in the public square, echo the shouts of "Viva Mexico! Long live Mexico!"

CHAPTER XV   JOSÉ MORELOS

ONE OF the young men who had joined Hidalgo was Father José Morelos. He was the son of a carpenter who died when the boy was very young. José Morelos grew up on the streets of Valladolid. He wanted to be a priest. At the very thought of such a thing people laughed and told him that his head was full of corn silk instead of brains. Nobody had ever heard of a street waif who wanted to be a priest.

José, however, still kept his dream. Even when he had grown tall and was driving mules for a living, he had not forgotten. One day he waited outside of the College of San Nicolás in Vallodolid. When Father Hidalgo, who was the rector, came out, he approached him to ask if he could study in the college. Was this possible for the son of a carpenter, who could pay his way only by mule driving? Father Hidalgo told him that he himself would teach the mule driver.

As the young student's education grew, his teacher realized that here was a man who had a fine mind and could make something of himself. It took José Morelos a long time to become a priest, for he had to spend many of his days on the road with his mules. But when he was thirty years old he finished his studies and became Father Morelos. He went to the country south of Mexico City. When he heard of the revolt led by Father Hidalgo, Morelos offered his services. At once Father Hidalgo sent him a commission as a trusted lieutenant and asked him to raise troops in his area of the south. With this letter he sent his blessings.

Morelos was a great man. Father Hidalgo, who passionately wanted freedom from Spain, believed that the people of Mexico could not govern themselves. He wished a European prince to become ruler' of Mexico. Morelos thought further than that. He wanted Mexico to become a republic and to be ruled by Mexicans. He offered to turn over his authority as leader to a congress. Morelos was an honest man, too. It was said that although much money passed through his hands, not a peso stuck to his fingers. He asked for laws to abolish slavery and to provide land and a chance for decent living for the Indians. He worked day and night, although he suffered from severe headaches and usually wore a handkerchief around his head to protect him from the sun.

When Father Hidalgo was defeated and executed, Morelos was winning victories in the south. Several wealthy men who owned large haciendas joined his army. One of his best officers was another priest, whose name was Matamoros. From 1810 to 1815, Morelos' army won battles over government troops and came close to taking the country itself.

Then Matamoros and several of the other leaders were captured and killed, while still others were bribed to betray Morelos. A new king came to the Spanish throne. Immediately more troops were sent from Spain to keep the Mexicans in order. The army of Morelos was defeated. José Morelos was captured by a former lieutenant in the Mexican Army who had accepted a bribe to betray his commander. As a priest Morelos was tried by the church and was called a heretic and a traitor to God, King and Pope. Like his friend and teacher, Father Hidalgo, Father Morelos was stripped of his priestly robes and executed.

Today the old city of Valladolid is called Morélia for the poor mule driver and priest. The state of Morelos is also named for him, for that is where he fought and won many battles. However, the revolutions did not end with his death. Many of the fighters fled into the wild mountains. There they lived with the hope of freeing Mexico from Spain. People still wanted freedom. They did not forget the two priests, Father Hidalgo and Father Morelos.

CHAPTER XVI   GENERAL SANTA ANNA

WHEN MORELOS was defeated, one of his chief leaders, Guerrero, continued to fight in the southern mountains. At the capital, in December, 1820, a Mexican monarchy was proclaimed by a general called Iturbide. A king for Mexico was to be brought over from Europe. The Spanish viceroy, unable to resist, recognized the new government. General Iturbide became more powerful because he controlled the Mexican Army. Instead of inviting a monarch from a royal family of Europe to rule Mexico, Iturbide, in 1822, declared himself Emperor of Mexico. His royal reign was short, for the country was without money in the treasury, and before long even the army had turned against the general. Three years later, a congress met and a republic was created. A constitution was adopted, giving people, for the first time, the right to vote. This meant little in reality, for the Indians could not read or write, and many of them had not yet learned the Spanish language.

A few years later Spain tried to reconquer Mexico, but her forces were defeated at Tampico by General Santa Anna. He called himself the "Napoleon of the West." Santa Anna was a man interested only in his own success. He was handsome, conceited and tricky. Within six months he had risen in rank from lieutenant to brigadier-general.

The general became powerful and wealthy. He lived on an estate near Vera Cruz. At that time Mexico still owned all of Texas, as well as California. When men from the United States began to move into Texas, General Santa Anna marched north with an army to drive them out. He overwhelmed and killed a gallant little band of men fighting desperately in the Alamo. But the "Napoleon of the West" was later defeated by Sam Houston and his pioneers. Santa Anna was captured hiding in some high grass, dressed in a blue shirt, white trousers and red carpet slippers. General Santa Anna, after signing away Texas, went home in disgrace.

Later French troops landed on the coast, and General Santa Anna was ordered again to fight. This was called the "French Pastry War" because France used the destruction of a French pastry shop during a riot in Mexico City as an excuse to invade Mexico and collect damages. In this battle one of the general's legs was shot off. Mexico settled the war by agreeing to pay the claims demanded. But Santa Anna was now a national hero. His friends brought his leg to Mexico City and, with great ceremony, buried it under a fine monument.

After that, General Santa Anna made himself the "Perpetual Dictator of Mexico." He admired pictures of the guards of the Russian Czar, with their great black beards. Since his own Indian guards had no bushy whiskers, Santa Anna made them wear false beards. Everywhere he went, Santa Anna acted like a royal prince. He rode in a sumptuous carriage, carrying his gamecocks with him.

The people, however, rebelled against the dictator and he was forced to abdicate. He went to Cuba but returned again to lead the army once

more when the United States declared war on Mexico in 1846. The Mexican general gathered an army of twenty-five thousand men and moved northward to battle General Zachary Taylor. Santa Anna wore a uniform weighted with golden embroidery and rode in a carriage drawn by eight mules, accompanied by his favorite fighting cocks to entertain him when he rested. Victory in the battle was claimed by the United States, but, after some fighting in a mountain pass, both forces withdrew. General Santa Anna went back to Mexico City, declaring himself a hero again.

He had no sooner arrived, though, than he received word that General Scott had come up from Vera Cruz with an army brought by ship. He was marching on Mexico City. Santa Anna manoeuvered his armies into defensive positions, but, after a siege in which the famous battle of Chapultepec took place, the city fell. A second time the general left Mexico in disgrace.

Santa Anna, the arrogant dictator, was never again able to return to the presidential palace. He had been president seven times. He lived thereafter in retirement and died unloved by his people. He was not an expert military leader, for under him Mexico lost to the United States, Texas, California, New Mexico and Arizona. As president, General Santa Anna had lived like a king and had brought the country to bankruptcy. Before he died, he heard that the people of Mexico City had removed the monument over his leg and roughly disposed of the only piece of their former leader that had been buried with honors.

CHAPTER XVII   THE BRAVE BOYS

JUAN, fourteen years old and slender, was one of the cadets in the old military school. He stood as erect as a statue in his gray military uniform, and he wore his blue tasseled cap as if he were a general. Some day he hoped to be a general in the Mexican Army, like his hero, Santa Anna. Yesterday he had watched the general riding his fine red horse jauntily through the courtyard of the Fort of Chapultepec. Juan could not imagine any time when this castle had not been a national stronghold. It had been the summer home of Moctezuma and then a presi-

dential palace. Now it was a fort and military college.

Juan stood quietly. In his ears rang the clang, clang of bells. Three days ago Father Hidalgo's bell of freedom had rung out in the plaza. That meant that the United States soldiers, the "gringoes," were about to attack. That also meant that every Mexican must take up arms to defend his country against another invasion. From the parapets of the castle, Juan could look down on the City of Mexico, with its long causeways through swampy ground where Lake Texcoco had once been. He heard the sound of other bells, clanging all over the city.

"How long, Juan?" asked his friend Edmundo. "When do you think they will attack?"

Juan pointed down and toward the west. There in a grove of ancient cypress trees they could see men and horses moving up. Field guns were rolling into position. Beyond was the King's Mill, El Molino del Rey, occupied by Mexican troops. Then the castle guns began to fire. The cadets drew back to make more room for gun crews going into action at the parapets. General Bravo, commander of the fort, strode to the battlements and saw the boys standing near the powder-streaked artillerymen. He commanded an officer to send the boys below. They marched inside, clattering stiffly down the stairs. The firing increased.

At dawn the next day, the cadets stood listening, pale and quiet. Shells came pounding from the efficient enemy artillery into the fort. Mexico had more men, but the "gringos" had more guns and better ones. There was a great shout. Juan forgot his orders. He ran for the stairs to the parapets, followed by the other cadets. They came out on a wild and bloody scene. The mine charge, laid in the ditch by the Mexicans around the fort, had not gone off. United States troops had crossed the ditch with scaling ladders. They climbed the high walls in a rush. Now they fought hand to hand on the fort.

The cadets grasped guns from fallen soldiers and began to fire at the enemy. Juan saw his friend Edmundo, surrounded by attackers in blue, wrap a Mexican flag about himself and leap from the parapet to death below rather than be captured.

And then, quite suddenly, it was over. Juan stared about him, holding an empty gun. Only a few of the cadets were prisoners. Most of them were dead. There was a strange silence. Juan knew, without being told, that the war was lost. He knew that the city was defeated, even though fighting would probably continue in the streets and on the causeways. He knew that his country had again been conquered.

CHAPTER XVIII   MAXIMILIAN

FOR FOURTEEN years after the war with the United States, Mexico was governed by Mexicans. A revolution, called the War of the Reform, had taken place in 1854, led by a lawyer, Benito Juárez, and a group of men who wished to give the people better living conditions and provide an honest government. But Santa Anna had left the country bankrupt. The Juárez government had angered the Catholic Church by taking away its huge wealth in lands. Some rich Mexicans in Paris persuaded the French Emperor to send an army to Mexico, and, in 1864, Maximilian, a young Austrian prince, was set up as Emperor of Mexico.

On the deck of a vessel, dropping anchor in the harbor at Vera Cruz, a young prince and princess stood, gazing eagerly at this strange land. Maximilian of Austria and his wife, Carlotta, knew little about the country they expected to rule. They had been told that troops of the French Emperor, Napoleon III, had invaded the country, and after one defeat had won a decisive battle at Puebla. They thought that the elected President of Mexico, Juárez, was a wild Indian who was scarcely more than a bandit. Maximilian knew that Juárez had fled to northern Mexico and set up a government in exile there. But this did not worry the young Emperor and Empress, for they thought that the Mexican people wanted them to come.

Consequently, when Carlotta and Maximilian went ashore and stepped into their carriage to be driven in triumph through the streets, they looked around them with dismay. The silence was frightening. There was no welcoming committee. Vera Cruz was like a city of the dead. There was not a human being on the streets. Only vultures walked on the cobblestones, picking at refuse. Every house was shuttered, and every man, woman and child stayed inside. Carlotta wept and begged to be taken back to the ship. Maximilian was pale, but he was determined to wait until the next day before making any decision.

The following morning, an official escort of troops arrived at Vera Cruz with welcoming guns and drums. Officers came to greet their new rulers and ordered the people onto the streets. But nobody came out. The Emperor and Empress rode past shuttered windows through a silent city up the road taken so long before by Cortez.

In Mexico City, the royal couple were given a suitable welcome. They were escorted by richly dressed officials to the palace. Maximilian and Carlotta soon learned to like Mexico. The Emperor had a real desire to improve the life of the poor. Every effort he made, however, was opposed by the landowners, for they wanted no weakening of their power.

It was not long before Maximilian found out that he had been given false information about Mexico. The people had not asked for him and did not want a foreign ruler. Benito Juárez was a man of brilliant mind and honest purpose. He had not given up and would never abandon his intention of driving the Austrian prince and his crowd from Mexico. Three years before, Juárez had issued his famous proclamation of reforms that confiscated vast rich lands of the church. Now the Pope expected Maximilian to give back the lands to the church. This, however, the Emperor refused to do.

Soon, Carlotta was the center of a gay society. She preferred the castle of Chapultepec to the palace in the plaza. She had it decorated as her summer palace with imported furniture and plants for the gardens. Maximilian had a broad avenue cut through the city from the castle to the great square. The old gardens and the palace of José de la Borda in the tropical town of Cuernavaca were bought by the Empress. There she spent many months of the year with her ladies in waiting. The Emperor traveled back and forth on the winding mountain road in a carriage drawn by twelve white mules.

To try to hold back criticism and please the society set, the Emperor and Empress gave elaborate parties. Since the government had no funds in the treasury, before long there was no more money for social affairs. Carlotta remained in Cuernavaca, and the Emperor and Empress became unpopular with the wealthy families responsible for bringing them to Mexico.

During the Civil War, the United States had not been able to pay any attention to her southern neighbor's difficulties. But when the war ended, the United States made it plain, by giving Juárez military aid, that she disliked having a European ruler in Mexico. Napoleon III, unwilling to have trouble with America, changed his mind about his Mexican venture and withdrew his army.

When Carlotta heard that the French Army was leaving, she could scarcely believe her ears. Surely, she thought, Napoleon would not desert them if he understood! So she took the next ship for France alone —her husband refusing to go with her. Maximilian must have known well enough that he could not win against the army of Juárez. But perhaps he thought he might hold out with a few loyal troops until Carlotta sent help from Europe? And if he could not win, he preferred to die in battle rather than go back across the seas, defeated.

Juárez was marching down from the north. When he reached Queretaro, his Mexican army supplied with United States guns, he met Maximilian. The Emperor did not die in battle. He was captured and held in prison for a time, while important people all over the world sent word begging Juárez not to execute him. Juárez said that since the Emperor had allowed Mexican prisoners to be shot, he, too, must die. On the day of execution, although Maximilian had to be helped from his bed in prison, for he was ill of fever, he walked without aid to the Hill of Bells, where, with his officers, he turned to face a firing squad.

CHAPTER XIX   EMPRESS CARLOTTA

As soon as the unhappy Carlotta reached France, she went at once to demand an audience with Napoleon III and the Empress Eugénie. They welcomed her politely but told her that it was no longer possible to support Maximilian. Napoleon did not wish to go to war with the

United States. He shrugged elegant shoulders and asked, "What can I do?"

Carlotta put her hand up to her aching head. Her memory was failing, and her mind was growing confused. Still she felt that she must get help. She would ask the Pope for aid. Carlotta went to Italy, but she was ill when she arrived. The Pope sent to Belgium for her brother, who came to take Carlotta to one of their father's estates. There she died in 1927 without knowing that her husband had been executed, more than half a century before, in Mexico.

CHAPTER XX   BENITO JUÁREZ

BENITO JUÁREZ, President of Mexico, was the first Indian ruler since Cuauhtémoc. Benito grew up in the lovely southern town of Oaxaca, where he lived in the streets most of the time, more often hungry than not. On Saturdays he wandered through the market, picking up a few centavos, whenever he could, by running errands. Sometimes he might make as much as a peso by carrying loads of black earthenware pottery or hand-loomed serapes made by the Indians. Often he sat in the evening, listening quietly to marimba players under the plaza trees or watching men leap and shout in the ancient feather dance of his people. Sometimes he went into the church to stand silently in the golden light streaming through the amber glass window.

As Benito grew older, a priest noticed the thoughtful black eyes under shaggy hair and offered to teach him. The boy learned quickly. He went to school and later studied law. And then, while still a young man, he became Governor of Oaxaca.

Benito Juárez was a good governor. People talked of him with respect because he was honest, and he saw that those who worked under him were honest. Where so many officials accepted bribes and made fortunes one way or another while in office, Juárez was never known to have taken a centavo beyond his salary. He was a quiet, thoughtful man, who always dressed in black, and wore a long black cape and high hat. He said little, but when he spoke, people listened.

Years before, after Santa Anna became dictator, Juárez was impris-

oned for opposing him. He soon escaped to New Orleans, however, where he made cigars for a living. He returned to Mexico when Santa Anna was displaced by a council of generals and was named Minister of Justice. His new laws provided for the sale of church property not used for worship and restricted the political power of the Catholic Church. Soon the church sympathizers revolted and civil war broke out. Juárez and his companions were hunted from town to town and many people were killed. It was at this point that his opponents imported Emperor Maximilian and the troops of Napoleon.

For several years, Juárez lived near the northern border of Mexico, going from place to place in his black carriage. In the resistance to the French, it was he who held out and finally defeated Maximilian. Before the Emperor was executed, Benito Juárez said, "It is not I, but the people of Mexico, who demand the death of Maximilian."

After the war with the French, Juárez undertook many reforms. He started schools to educate Indian children and reduced the size of the army. This angered the officers who tried to start revolts. Juárez also met resistance from the church. He was so opposed by powerful land-owners that he was unable to give out much land to the people who needed it. Indians still worked on the haciendas, the huge estates of the wealthy, much as they had done a hundred years before. The people of Mexico, however, wanted to be governed by Mexicans, not by a foreign power.

Even though Juárez had little time to carry out his plans for his country—he died shortly after he was re-elected to the presidency in 1871—he was greatly loved and mourned.

CHAPTER XXI   THE ROMANTIC BANDIT

IN MEXICO stories are told and sung and often woven into festival dances. Some of these are about real figures in Mexican history, while others are only romantic legends. The evil Malinche appears in many of them as a traitor to her country and Empress Carlotta as a heroine.

Of all the gay, romantic heroes, Lorenzo the bandit is the most popular.

Long ago, on the road from Mexico City to Vera Cruz, travelers bumping over mule tracks glanced fearfully up at steep mountainsides or into wild forests. As they traveled, they listened and kept their pistols cocked. This was bandit country. Here the most exciting outlaw of the 1800's, Augustin Lorenzo, waylaid his victims and took their gold and silver and whatever jewels or expensive ornaments they had.

It is said that on this highway there once rode a most beautiful señorita. She was traveling back to her father's hacienda after a visit to the city. Now, when Augustin Lorenzo saw this girl, he forgot his plans for robbery. He was so overcome that he allowed the lady to ride on, unmolested. Afterward he could not sleep. He could no longer keep his thoughts on robbery. The following month he even neglected to steal a fortune in silver, hauled slowly along the road on the backs of a hundred mules.

One night Lorenzo and his men mounted their horses and rode to the hacienda. There the bandit found his señorita and sweeping her to his horse, he carried her away to his mountain camp. Then, as music echoed and feasting began, a captive priest prepared for the wedding ceremony. Suddenly, like a clap of thunder, out of the forests rushed the father of the girl, with his sons and his friends and his cowhands. A great battle took place there in front of the thatched roofs of the bandit huts. Lorenzo was killed by the enraged father, and the señorita was taken home.

Lorenzo, of course, did not really die. He lives on in the famous carnival of Augustin Lorenzo, celebrated every year in the city of Puebla. A thousand men assemble in battle groups. There are the Apaches, dressed in brilliant feathered skirts and headdresses. They wear shirts of pink and purple, with beads and feathers and mirrors sewed on them. There are the Zapadores, in blue uniforms and black beards. Then come the French Zouaves, in blue and red costumes, with loaves of French bread on their hats, carrying guns and swords. The mountain people wear black shirts and white cotton trousers and carry stuffed animals and machetes. They run around like clowns during the festival.

For five days and nights, the city celebrates the carnival, with dancing, fireworks and fun. Then Augustin Lorenzo, in splendid dress, rides into town with a white plume waving on his hat. He calls on a youth, dressed as a girl in white, seated in an upstairs window. This "señorita" leaps from the window down to a horse and gallops with Lorenzo to a thatched hut. There the father and his men appear and the mock battle takes place. The wedding ends with the death of the bandit and the triumph of the angry father.

CHAPTER XXII   CORN

YOLANDA who was the small daughter of José and Consuelo, worked
hard in the cornfields with her mother. Her little brothers were yet too
small to work, and it took much hard labor to pay the rents on their field.
When the time came to take the payment to the patron, Yolanda went
with her father while her mother stayed home with the little ones.

Yolanda helped her father stack and tie the corn shocks, and she
gathered the ears into the big sacks and her smaller one. She looked
sadly at the pile of corn left for the family, for it was not enough to keep
them in tortillas for the rest of the year. But she said nothing. Instead
she filled her own small sack and knelt down so that José could swing it
upon her thin shoulders. Then she watched her father raise the big sack
to his own shoulders. It was so heavy that it bowed him almost double
as he adjusted the tump line around his forehead.

Yolanda followed him, and they went slowly along the road to the
hacienda. There they stood in line with the other farmers in their white

cotton trousers and shirts and big straw hats. Not many women and girls were there. José poured his corn into a measuring basket and the foreman wrote the amount in a book. While he marked down her corn, Yolanda straightened her aching back. Suddenly all of the farmers bowed as a horse galloped up. A man in a black suit trimmed with silver buttons, carrying a riding whip and wearing a magnificent sombrero, pulled in his horse. The hacendado, or landowner, spoke, using many words that the girl didn't understand.

Yolanda followed the others to the road. "What did the hacendado say, Father?"

"He said that we must bring more corn for our rent next time."

"Father, how can we? We have worked so hard this year for our corn."

"I do not know, Yolanda. We will have less corn for ourselves then. If we do not pay more, our field will no longer be ours. The patron will take it over, as he did Pancho's last year. I do not know—your mother will burn a candle in the church and—perhaps," his voice dropped very low as they walked in the dusty road, "perhaps to that stone image in the big field of Pietro's, the one that has been there so long—perhaps we might make an offering of flowers to it. And we must work."

Yolanda thought of Indian corn, of the yellow grains that meant life to her and her family. If the patron took over José's land, then they would work for the patron. She sighed, for her family had owned this little plot longer than anybody could remember. Even if they worked for the patron, they must still grow corn and till corn and cut the yellow ears of corn. When they came into the windowless adobe hut, she sighed again. Her mother was baking tortillas, thin and white, on the stone over the little charcoal fire. Yolanda had only poverty to look forward to the rest of her life.

WITH THE passing of the years after the death of Juárez, conditions did not change very much. The Indians lived as they had always lived, raising their corn, cutting sugar cane on big plantations, weaving mats, making bowls and often going hungry.

After Juárez there were many presidents. Some ran the country a few months; others a year or so. General Porfirio Diaz, who had been an officer under Juárez in the War of the Reform, remained in office longer than any other. He was the most skillful military man in Mexican history and was well liked by the hacendados. His chief aim, he said, was to "enforce peace." When he first came to office in 1876, he did not oppose the reform laws of Juárez. He just failed to enforce them. Gradually the church took back its lands and opened schools taught by priests and nuns. Diaz interested foreign investors in Mexican enterprises and brought in money from England and the United States to build railroads and schools. He was slowly modernizing Mexico.

Yet the Indians became even poorer. Small plots of land on which they grew corn or beans in the good soil of the valleys were lost to them. They were forced onto the more barren lands higher up steep mountainsides. The rich valleys and wide grazing acres for cattle went to wealthy men, some Mexican, some foreign. Slowly the Indians became restive.

To keep peace and maintain order, Diaz organized a rural police force of brave, ruthless men. Many of them had been bandits. These rurales dressed in tight buckskin trousers and fancy shirts, with short jackets embroidered in silver. They wore big sombreros weighted with gold and silver decorations and scarlet serape blankets folded across the shoulder. They carried pistols and guns and knives to subdue the barefoot Indians. The rurales rode fine prancing horses and some carried guitars to serenade dark-eyed señoritas. But they were cruel to any poor man who committed the smallest offense. People hated the rurales.

By bribery and crooked elections, General Diaz stayed in office as a

virtual dictator. He also kept in office the men he liked and who served him well. Mexico became a country run mainly by old men. Young men, well educated for political careers, found no such careers open to them. They resented the dictatorship and wanted a change. They were also angry because Diaz allowed foreigners to buy vast lands and own mines and oil fields.

When Diaz was eighty years old, he celebrated his birthday by giving the most elaborate party ever held in the palace. At the dinner his young and charming wife, Carmen, was as gracious as a queen. Outside in the plaza, Diaz supporters shouted gaily. Sixteen bands played, and fireworks spurted like comets across the sky. But like the comet in the time of Moctezuma, who had lived on this very spot, the fireworks comets were signs of trouble for the man in the palace. The birthday of President Diaz came at just about the time of the Mexican Independence Day. This was 1910, exactly a hundred years after the priest, Father Hidalgo, had called out for freedom from Spain.

Beyond the lighted plaza, people all over Mexico were crying for land, for bread and for honest elections. Nothing that the old dictator did could quiet the unrest. He had himself re-elected president for another term. Revolt ran like a grass fire across the land. People were listening to a small man named Francisco Madero. Diaz had Madero arrested, but the little man with the nervous smile looked so unimportant to the dictator, that he allowed him out on bail. Madero received support everywhere—from the wild bandit of the north, Pancho Villa—to the peasant leader, Zapata, in the south.

Because of the unrest, General Diaz left hurriedly for France. There he died a few years later, while Mexico boiled with revolution. Diaz had "enforced peace" in his country for many years. He had also brought in railroads and oil wells and foreign investors. He had made Mexico a country recognized by the rest of the world as important. But he had not brought a better life to the great numbers of Indians who wanted land of their own.

ON THE eighth of June, 1911, people packed and jammed themselves into the railroad station of Mexico City in a great crowd, which overflowed into the street. They waited, talking, laughing, sometimes singing. Vendors sold tortillas and fruit. Babies wailed in the crush, and feet shuffled back and forth in the Mexican sandals called huaraches.

A train pulled slowly into the station. From somewhere in the crowd a cry came, and then they all shouted, "Viva Madero! Viva Mexico!"

The train bumped to a halt. A step was placed before a special car, and a little man put his foot on it. At that moment an ominous sound seemed to swell and grow. The earth slowly began to sway. People cried out, afraid. They covered their faces with their hands. An earthquake was a bad omen.

They did not run, however, and there was no panic. When the earthquake stopped, Madero, who was a small, thin man, spoke in a high shrill voice that could scarcely be heard. Yet the people shouted, "Viva Madero! Viva Mexico!"

They did not have to hear him speak to know that he was an upright man, who wanted to make things better for them. Madero was elected by an honest vote, but trouble followed for him at once.

The revolutionary leader in the south, Emiliano Zapata, who had given Madero support, demanded land for the people. A nephew of Diaz, plotting with a General Huerta to take over the government, was stirring up revolt in the army. Madero made foreign owners of oil wells angry by taxing them. Revolt broke out, and there was fighting in the streets of Mexico City. The leading generals and officers of the army, commanded by Bernardo Reyes, turned against Madero. At seven o'clock on a February morning, as señoritas and their mothers, in Sunday silks with black lace mantillas on their heads, walked across the great square to early mass, they saw men running toward them. When they approached the ancient cathedral, placed on Aztec temple ruins by Cor-

tez, they heard shots and ran screaming into the church. Troops were firing on the presidential palace. They were answered by the guns of the palace guard. More than two hundred churchgoers, men, women and children, as well as many soldiers, were killed. General Huerta took no open part in this revolt, which lasted ten days, but when it ended, he pledged his loyalty to the president. Madero made the mistake of giving him command of the government troops.

The cruel Huerta, allied with the nephew of Diaz, revolted against Madero. In Mexican towns and cities sellers of single-sheet newspapers did a rushing business. Men would buy them and then, with their lips tight, walk away, dropping the papers. Others would pick them up. Although they could not read printed words, they could read this news. Here was a picture by an artist named Posada. The picture told the story. Madero had been murdered. Huerta was the new President of Mexico.

CHAPTER XXV   POSADA

IN THE streets of Monterey, in northern Mexico, people stood laughing as they looked at a political cartoon, printed on a small sheet of paper. In the town of Vera Cruz, men and women smiled as they read the many verses of a ballad printed on a long, narrow strip of paper.

"That's a fine picture. Who made it?"

"Who else but Posada? He makes these pictures by cutting blocks of wood. Who else but Posada?"

From north to south, from east to west, people knew the pictures of Posada.

Guadalupe Posada was born in 1864, in the town of León. When he was twenty-two, he went to Mexico City and began making woodcuts for a publishing firm. He cut his pictures directly on blocks of wood, in reverse, and they were then printed. Posada worked hard and spent most of his life in the little printer's shop.

Late strollers in the street would often see the artist, his head bent over his work table. After a while Posada developed a way of using metal plates and etching his pictures with acid, instead of cutting them

on wood. This saved him time, for making woodcuts was a slow process. After that the number of his pictures increased until the broadsides and handbills that carried his work were known and loved all over the country.

The artist lived through two revolutions, and he made many cartoons and engravings showing the events of the time. Even today, after his death, one may buy a song illustrated with the pictures of Posada, worn but still clear and beautiful, still printed over and over. The picture might show lovers in a park, or men drinking in a café, or dancing in fantastic costumes at a carnival. It might be a picture of a bullfight in the great city arena on a Sunday afternoon. It seemed as if all of the life of Mexico went into the pictures that came from the little printshop of Guadalupe Posada.

To THE Mexican, a bullfight is the greatest of all entertainments. Every town has a small bull ring. Every village will put on a bullfight in an open field, even if the bull is old and gentle and the matador is a young fellow with a red cotton cloth for a cloak. Every little boy plays bullfighter, and great matadors are national heroes.

A time came, however, during the long dictatorship of General Diaz when bullfights were not enough to take the minds of the poor from hardship and hunger. They must have more land. How else could they grow corn for tortillas? In 1910 they were desperate enough to follow a leader and to fight. In the south they were ready to follow Emiliano Zapata to the cries of,

"Land and freedom!"
"The land belongs to him who works it with his hands."

Zapata told his men that and they believed him. They came from their little fields, from their mud huts and from their mountain wilderness. They came to join in the fight that he led against the hacendados.

Emiliano Zapata himself was not a peon, a farm worker who had no land at all. He was a ranchero, or tenant owner of a small ranch, one that he worked himself. He grew his own corn, and he had a yoke of oxen. His little ranch was in the state of Morelos, near the town of Cuautla, which is located in the sugar cane area. Zapata was a thin man with black hair, a big black moustache and piercing dark eyes. He sometimes dressed in black like any other ranchero, with tight trousers, little jacket, large hat and a scarf of red or purple. But when he worked he dressed in the white cotton clothes of the poor farmer. Some said that Zapata was the finest horseman in all Morelos, and others said in all Mexico, which is a land of expert horsemen.

Zapata was filled with hatred for those who took from a farmer his little piece of land. In the time of General Diaz, there were many ways of taking the farms away from the poor. Even though a farmer's family

had ploughed his land since Aztec days, if he did not have a piece of paper—a deed—which he could not read, he could be thrown off. Zapata wanted nothing for himself. He wanted land for the Indians. He was part Indian in blood, and this revolution was by the Indians and for the Indians.

Led by Zapata on his white horse, Lightning, these poor people came down with their machetes or guns on a hacienda, killed the owner and overseers and opened the safe. From the safe they took the deeds and burned them. Then they returned home to plough or plant. Zapata and his guard had a camp in a wild mountain pass called Wolf Canyon. When he wanted to destroy a hacienda, he could rouse thousands of farmers and bring them together in a few hours. When the job was done, they disappeared into villages and mountains. Nobody could tell whether a man dropping seeds into furrowed rows was a zapatista or not.

When Diaz fled and Madero became president, Zapata met him in the town of Cuernavaca in the zócalo, or square. There they agreed to join forces. But Zapata ended the talk by shouting,

"If you do not give the people land, I will provide a bullet for you and one for each of the other traitors."

It was General Huerta, not Zapata, however, who provided the bullet for Madero. When the revolution failed, Zapata disappeared into the mountains. He emerged from time to time to burn a sugar mill or ranch.

Zapata killed hacendados on sight and destroyed their property, but to the poor and the dispossessed, Zapata was a hero, whom they adored and protected. They could hide him from the rurales and keep his secrets, yet they could not protect him from treachery.

When Huerta became dictator, a movement was started to avenge the death of Madero and put in a better man than Huerta. Carranza, a northern governor, took the leadership and gathered an army. The other leader in the north was Pancho Villa, a bandit, while Carranza was a wealthy landowner. At first they joined forces, then, later, they fought separately as rivals, and finally, after Huerta had been defeated and had fled, they fought each other. Villa and Zapata became so successful that they joined forces and entered Mexico City. Then Carranza, with Obregón as his general, defeated Villa. To capture Zapata, however, Carranza had to resort to treachery.

One of Carranza's officers pretended that he was going over to Zapata and would bring guns with him. Zapata, who had fought nine years, was in need of guns. When he came to town from the mountains to meet the officer, he was shot down without a chance to defend himself.

The people say that Zapata is not dead. When the night is dark and the wind blows cold from the snowy tops of the volcanoes, a sound can be heard. Indians sleeping on thin straw mats in their adobe huts declare that they can hear the hoofbeats and the cry, "Land and Liberty!" And at dusk when men plod in from the fields swinging their machetes, weary from a day of cutting sugar cane, some claim that they have seen Zapata. Others say that he pounds through the village square on his big white horse, Lightning, coming back to lead them again in their constant struggle for corn and land.

CHAPTER XXVII

THE MEN of Tepoztlán laid aside their machetes. The village was ready to celebrate carnival, for this was the week before Lent. It was in a time of revolution, too, and it was the country of the zapatistas. At any moment the command might come down from the hills, causing every man to pull his gun from its hiding place under the red tile roof, or pick up his machete and slip away for a raid. But no word had come for some time, and the village always celebrated carnival week with a three-day dance of the village men who were members of a club called the Chinelos dancers.

As Nacho ran quickly from his home through the village, he held most carefully, in clean hands, a gay satin costume. Glancing down at it from time to time, he remembered that he was now ten years old and that this robe would undoubtedly fit him quite as well as it would young Jorge, who was to wear it today in the carnival dance.

Nacho's father had been killed several years before, and now Rosa, Nacho's mother, made costumes for other people. Hanging at home was Father's robe and mask and huge silken hat covered with embroidery and tiny mirrors. Father had once led a group of the village Chinelos dancers, but Nacho must wait until he was a man to wear this costume.

The streets were filled with excited noises, sights and smells. Old women had set up their charcoal fires and were cooking beans and sauces and tortillas. Boys were setting off firecrackers in the dust. Indians from far up the encircling mountains were plodding down into the little valley, leading their burros, to see the fun.

Nacho heard the sound of guns and a burst of music from drums and trumpets. Two of the groups must be starting from different parts of the village now. He ran to the cantina, where he was to meet Jorge, the leader of the dancers. When Nacho saw the men in their red, green and blue satin robes, huge hats and bearded masks in hand, he began to gasp out an apology for being late. But big Jorge did not let him finish.

"Quickly, Nacho," he called, "get into costume. Little Jorge dropped a firecracker on his foot and burned it badly. We must have a boy to help lead the troop. Quick now—pronto."

Nacho could not speak for excitement. He thrust the robe over his head and took the small mask with painted face and black beard from Jorge. Then as the men began to march and fire guns into the air, he fell in behind them with Jorge. The other dancers followed, with the band bringing up the rear, drums beating, trumpets blaring loudly.

At the plaza, the other two groups were already dancing in the center. Suddenly the music behind Nacho changed from marching to jumping music. Nacho jumped and turned and jumped and whirled. One of the dancers thrust a perfume atomizer into his hands. He gaily squirted perfume at every girl who came near. The throb of the drums, the blare of the horns rang in his ears. Around the dusty square, whirl, jump, jump, jump, turn! The monotonous tune went tirelessly on and on.

Nacho danced for hours, until he was dizzy and exhausted. Then big Jorge thrust a few centavos into his hand and motioned to him to drop out with the boy leaders of the other groups. The three boys bought enchiladas, which were corn pancakes dripping with chili sauce, and sat and watched the dance as they ate. Stars twinkled above the old Aztec pyramid on a mountaintop overlooking the village of Tepoztlán, and moonlight touched the dome of the stone church built by Spaniards.

Nacho went home at last, weary but happy. He would not wear this costume again, for little Jorge would certainly stay away from firecrackers and have his chance to dance next carnival time. But Nacho was proud of having been a Chinelos dancer. When he could put on his father's robes, he would dance for three days and nights, the way all Chinelos dancers did.

CHAPTER XXVIII   PANCHO VILLA

IN NORTHERN Mexico, at another fiesta, everybody in a crowd on the plaza stared at one man as he strolled about. When he laughed, his roar even shook the little booths where straw dolls hung. The sound sent small boys scuttling out of his way when they caught a glimpse of his low-slung pistols. Everybody knew him. This was Pancho Villa, the bandit.

Like Zapata, Villa was a great horseman, but, unlike Zapata, he was a big, heavy man. He wore an outfit made for a life in the saddle, with huge spurs and a large felt sombrero. His name had not always been Pancho Villa. When he was a boy, he was called Doroteo Arango. As he grew older, he heard stories of a famous legendary bandit who was said to give to the poor after robbing the rich—one Pancho Villa. Young Arango took the name of the bandit. If anyone called him anything else, the new Villa pulled out his pistol and shot him.

Pancho Villa had a remarkable ability to draw other adventurers into his band. He enjoyed robbing, cattle rustling, fighting and leading an army. He hated rich landowners as much as Zapata did, but at first he was not a real revolutionary like Zapata. Yet Villa was often on the side of the poor. He listened to their troubles and tried to help them by giving them stolen cattle and goods.

Villa rode a great black horse named Lucifer. It was said that Lucifer was so smart that he could find food for his master when needed. It was also said that the horse could pick up his saddle in his teeth and bring it to Villa. And Lucifer would warn the men if an enemy was near.

When he joined the army of Francisco Madero, Pancho Villa changed from a cattle thief and bandit to a revolutionary leader. From that time on, for a number of years, he took part in one war after another. First, he fought beside Carranza, and then he fought against him and lost.

Villa's army was a ragged mass of peons, who moved on foot after his horsemen, or rode from battle to battle, clinging to the tops of railroad cars, as well as inside coaches. Along the long line of railroad, stretching through the brown northern hills, and through cactus-studded desert moved the trains. The men of Villa's strange army sang their rowdy cockroach song, *La Cucaracha*, and twanged on guitars. Boxcars were jammed with soldiers and women and children, too, for Villa's men brought along their families.

These women, wrapped in their colored shawls, gathered corn in the fields where they camped and cooked for their men. Children stripped the country bare of fruit and vegetables. And Villa's rustlers and his wild brigade of Yaqui Indians killed cattle wherever they wanted meat. The women took care of the sick and wounded, dragging men from battlefields, for there were no doctors and nurses.

Some years later, after Villa had again become a cattle thief and bandit and had made raids across the border of the United States, General Pershing was sent into Mexico with American troops to catch him. Villa, however, only roared with laughter and disappeared into the barren hills. The United States soldiers had to return without him.

At last, a new president, General Obregón, who had led the army of Carranza, decided to end the cattle-stealing raids of the villistas. Since no army, United States or Mexican, could catch the big Pancho Villa, Obregón thought of a new idea to quiet him. He simply asked the former leader to retire from raiding and offered him a good ranch to live on.

Villa called his men and said to them, "From now on I do not wish to kill any more. Come on, señors, we will go back to the land."

They went with him. However, after a few quiet years Villa was murdered. Nobody knows who shot him or why, but the people admire brave men in Mexico. So Pancho Villa has become a legend, and they say that the big bandit with the huge cartridge belt and pistols still laughs in a roar that shakes the mountains. They say that he rides his black Lucifer through cactus-covered hills—never to be caught by the federal soldiers, they say. Not Pancho Villa!

CHAPTER XXIX   PEACE ON THE LAND

FROM 1911 to 1926 revolution kept Mexico in a condition of violence
and turmoil. In the north, Pancho Villa was master of much of the
country. In the south, Zapata was fighting his own war. The central
government had first one and then another leader. When the people
heard that Emiliano Zapata was coming to occupy the City of Mexico,
they locked themselves into their houses, trembling. The zapatistas in
their humble cotton clothes only went quietly about the city, doing no

harm, just asking politely for food. After a short time they returned to their homes in the south.

Under Obregón, peace came to Mexico. Fighters hid their guns and went back to work. Revolutionary songs, such as *Adelita* and *Valentina* and *La Cucaracha* were no longer heard around campfires. The new president tackled the problems of land and education. Some villages received land taken from the large haciendas. Many new schools were built by the government and teachers were trained and agricultural colleges started.

Then Obregón's friend, Calles, was elected president. He had been a school teacher before serving in the Obregón government. Calles and his friends became very wealthy while he was in office, but they also encouraged the building of factories, railroads and roads. The government began important systems of irrigation and water control, to save the soil from erosion and more land was distributed to farmers. The government's policy also encouraged better working conditions and the

growth of labor unions in the factories and industries.

As political leader of the country, Calles, although no longer president, chose Lázaro Cárdenas to run for the highest office in the land. Cárdenas was a new kind of president, for he did not enrich himself when he came to office, and he did not deliberately create a group of rich followers. He was serious in his promise to the people when he said that he would try to bring about reforms. He wanted to provide more land, schools and better conditions for city workers. Cárdenas did not attempt to keep foreign investors out of the country, but he wanted higher wages for the Mexican workers in the companies owned by foreigners.

Since the time of Cárdenas, many changes have taken place in Mexico. Men still plough the fields behind slow oxen, but some have tractors and trucks. Huge Brahman cattle with humps on their backs have been brought in to improve the native stock of cattle. New factories are making Mexican products, and Mexican canned goods are coming into the stores. Schools are filled with children learning Spanish, even in remote Indian villages high in the mountains or down in the tropical jungles. Tourists come by thousands every year. They like to see the folk dances, fiestas and bullfights. They go away with pottery, shawls, blankets and baskets.

Roads to the larger towns are paved for cars and busses. Yet many things are the same. The majority of the Mexicans are still poor. They still crowd markets with their flowers and fruit, as in the days of the Aztec Empire. Roads, railroads and airplanes are making rapid changes in Mexican life. Yet Mexico is becoming ever more aware that its ancient culture has a beauty and a value of which it can be proud. And Mexicans are learning more and more about the pyramids and temples and the life of their ancestors.

In the state of Vera Cruz there have been found enormous stone heads, covered for centuries by trailing jungle vines. They were carved by an unknown tribe living in that region long before the Aztecs came. Aztec ruins of temples and tombs around the Valley of Mexico, in Mexico City and in the ancient city of Tula to the north have been opened up. The early races had many artists working in stone, but the purpose of the great stone heads that they made has not yet been discovered. Who made them and what they were for remain mysteries.

Near Mexico City is a field of lava, miles wide, known as the pedregal, and in the pedregal is the oldest pyramid in Mexico. It is called Cuicuilo, which means "Place of Song and Color." It was found by digging through a top layer of lava stone to an even older layer beneath. In and around the Mexico City area are many temples of the Aztecs and Toltecs with remarkable stone figures of their gods. Farther south, the two mountain ranges that extend along the country meet in the state of Oaxaca. The town of Oaxaca, near the ruins of the temples of the Zapotec and Mixtec tribes, was built in Spanish colonial days, but the ruined temples and tombs of Monte Albán and Mitla are much older.

When the tombs of Monte Albán were opened, more treasures were found than in any other excavation on the American continent. There were beads, earrings and belt ornaments, as well as a golden breastplate, carved bones, jade, obsidian and ancient shells. Some of the necklaces were strung with the teeth of wolves and alligators, and there were skulls covered with mosaic patterns in turquoise. These were the possessions of the early Indian priests in the days when Monte Albán was a sacred religious city of the Zapotecas tribe.

As Monte Albán fell into ruin and was gradually covered with grass-grown earth, Spaniards ruled Mexico in the city of the Aztecs and brought in their customs to become part of Mexican life. One of these—the bullfight—has long been the national Mexican sport. The first bull-fight was held in Mexico City in the plaza seven years after Cortez had subdued the Aztecs, and now the city has the largest ring in the world.

Every Sunday afternoon the bullfighters, in brilliant costumes, toreros, banderilleros and mounted picadors parade into the ring behind a rider in ancient traditional Spanish dress. The huge ring is filled with people waiting to see the courage and skill of a man pitted against the strength of a dangerous animal. The smallest mistake made by a bull-fighter may mean his death. Horses are sometimes killed by the bull, and the bull himself nearly always dies.

To all Mexicans the bullfighter is a hero, and each year many young men enter the hundred bull rings in the country, hoping to receive some day the greatest honor of all—the ear and tail of the bull presented in the ring after the kill.

PAINTING is the greatest of the arts in Mexico today, and more has been achieved in painting than in music and writing, though these have their important names, too. All the world knows, however, of Mexican art— art as distinctly Mexican as the tortilla and the serape. Some of this art is the work of men of the Indian races, some is by Mexicans who are not Indian at all. What they have in common is a simplicity, dignity and charm that are the spirit of Mexico.

Art began in Mexico with the early Indians. By the time the Spaniards arrived, native arts were everywhere, gay and lovely as well as useful, whether fashioned of clay, straw or leather.

The Spaniards brought with them Spanish painting and Spanish tiles, Moorish crafts and designs. For many years Mexican painters imitated the Spanish methods and styles. In recent years Mexican painters have studied in Paris and have returned to develop in their own country a school of painting that is now world-renowned, modern in method and yet still uniquely Mexican.

The great paintings of modern Mexico have been done by men who sought something Mexican in subject and expression. Many of these men lived through a revolution. Their personal experiences were of battles and bloodshed. They have shown these battles and the people of the revolutions in their canvases, their block prints and lithographs. And when the government gave them walls to paint on, they created great compositions showing many phases of the struggle of the Mexican people during their long and exciting history. Nowhere else in the world can the people of a country see so much of their own story told pictorially on the big walls of their public buildings. Mexican painters who are known throughout the world are Diego Rivera, David Siqueiros, Rufino Tomayo, Miguel Covarrubias, and José Orozco.

One of the greatest painters of Mexico was José Clemente Orozco. He came of a Spanish family and was born in Zapotlán, state of Jalisco,

in 1883. Orozco attended public schools in Mexico City and graduated from the National Agricultural School of Mexico. He also studied mathematics and architectural drawing in the School of Fine Arts. Then, although he had lost one hand in an accident when he was a child, he decided to become a painter.

Orozco painted in oils and made lithographs and drawings. But, most important of all, he painted murals on walls. He trained himself in a way of painting in fresco similar to that of the old masters of Europe, and yet somewhat different. In the great patio of the National Preparatory School in Mexico City, he did murals that tell the Mexican story— *Ancient Races, Franciscan and Indian, Conqueror-Builder, Cortez and Malinche.* In the Industrial School at Orizaba he did a huge wall, twenty-four feet wide by thirty-five feet high—*Social Revolution.*

In the nineteen-thirties Orozco came to the United States, where he produced some of his best work. One mural with a great central figure, called *Prometheus,* is at Pomona College, California. Others are in the

New School in New York City and still others at Dartmouth College.

When Orozco was just a boy, he said that his ambition was "to bring one grain of sand to the future monument of Mexico." Now the paintings and murals of Orozco are world-famous, and people from all the world go to the public buildings in Mexico to see them.

Other Mexican artists have painted religious subjects—the life of St. Francis or the legend of the Virgin of Guadalupe. They also paint Mexican heroes—Cuauhtémoc suffering tortures at the hands of Cortez—Father Hidalgo ringing the liberty bell at Dolores—Father Casas and other good priests helping Indian children. In pictures may be seen the stern, dark face of Juárez, or Morelos standing like a rock, or Pancho Villa charging across the scene on his black horse, Lucifer. Emiliano Zapata rides on a wall through painted sugar cane fields at the head of a group of ragged cotton-clad farmers.

Mexican painters will show pictures of straight brown women in their blue shawls and men with machetes and wide sombreros. They paint the children, fat babies looking solemnly out with round black eyes, or older, thinner children, school boys and girls, street waifs, bootblacks, and market boys—all eager, quick and friendly. They paint Mexican life and Mexicans as they were before the conquerors came and as they are today.

THE CUERNAVACA market was a place of good smells to Mario. To others it was a place of color, with piles of red chili peppers, yellow lemons, green squash, beans, corn and tomatoes. To many the best parts were the stalls piled high with bright crockery bowls and vases and plates. Others were attracted to baskets stacked in great heaps and cotton skirts and blouses, embroidered and painted.

To Mario, it was a place of wonderful smells. He was an Indian errand boy, one of the small youths who waited around in the market to help housewives or their maids carry home bags of food. Today he was especially anxious to make some extra pesos, for it was his mother's name day and he wanted to bring something special for dinner. He counted the coins in his pocket—enough for a day's work, but not enough for a feast. Mario's eyes searched for his best patroness, who had not yet been to market that day, but he did not see her.

"Boy," called a tall American señora, "come here quickly. It is late."

Mario ran, pushing through the crowd of chattering women, all bargaining now for cheap prices since it was near closing time. He followed the señora, who bought and bought, until Mario could scarcely be seen for the paper sacks stuffed with fruit and vegetables. The señora bought two chickens at the stall but refused to take the last one there. The seller brought the price down to half, since it was a small chicken and the last one. Mario pushed along with her. This was an American señora, and she moved very, very fast.

"Here, boy," she called, "this way." Mario moved fast, too.

He came out of the market buildings, shoved his way through the market in the street and around the corner. There stood a shiny car. Mario's heart sank. He would not get much for carrying bags so short a distance, he thought. Mario placed the food inside the car.

"Muchas gracias," said the señora and dropped money in his hand. Then she drove swiftly away, honking her horn loudly, sending people

and dogs running. Mario gasped. She had given him three pesos! The usual price was half a peso. With the money he already had he could buy that chicken and also some hot chili powder and chocolate and nuts for the mole sauce—and, yes, even a few pan dulce or cookies. He ran so fast now that the lined-up tortilla women called angrily at him for pushing their baskets. The one last chicken was still there. With his own package Mario started out.

"Mario!" called his regular patroness. "Will you carry my package?"

"Not today, señora," answered Mario, his face breaking into a smile. "I am sorry. Now I go home to a feast dinner in honor of my mother's name day."

As he ran out Mario sniffed once more the rich market odor—the smell of corn baking to thin tortillas, of hot grease frying, of beans and onions and tomatoes and tropical fruits. There was the smell of animals, of ropes and straw and of flowers everywhere. This was the smell of Mexico.

Mario heard the sound of Mexico, too, but he was so used to it that he did not notice the donkeys braying, roosters crowing, dogs barking, fireworks popping and always brassy church bells ringing, day and night. There was the sound of hooves clopping on cobbles and of the

soft slapping of sandals in the dust. There was the sound of women's hands patting tortillas of corn meal into shape. There was a squealing of pigs and a gobbling of turkeys.

Mario saw Mexico. He saw, without noticing, the snowy cone of the volcano, old Popo, as if caught in a frame between the modern gas station and the ancient gray stone palace built by Cortez on the square. He ran across the three plazas, together in the center of the town, each next to the other. He saw the bandstand, the fountain and the handsome old trees. He saw tourists gazing spellbound at this lovely town and Indians from distant mountains sitting on the street selling clay angels. Lights were winking on. He saw boys and girls in their evening walk around the largest square, boys strolling one way, girls the other. He saw the soft dusk, a violet light on the hills, and the rosy afterglow of sunset. But he did not notice anything in particular as he ran home. He was just a part of Mexico.

All over Mexico, public squares were drawing people out of Spanish homes, out of adobe huts, to listen to the music of the band. The public plaza is the very heart of Mexican life. Here revolutionary leaders have met politicians to discuss armistice. Here guns have spattered bullets and men have fallen in the dust, sending flocks of birds screaming out of the old trees. Here boy courts girl, and Indians sit on benches and on the ground to eat their tortillas.

Here wandering musicians called *mariachis* sing and play at café tables for the customers. Craftsmen sell their shawls and wallets and silver trinkets and, on November first, candies made in the shape of skeletons for the Fiesta of the Day of the Dead. Here fireworks pop and generals make speeches, and girls sometimes dance a fandango. Here the brown faces of Indians from many tribes break into friendly smiles. And it is easy to remember Moctezuma in his crown of green quetzal feathers, waiting for the Plumed Serpent god to return to bring good fortune to Mexico.